Through Her Words
I Live

Finding My Strength
Through Rediscovery

Jessica N. Waller

CONTENTS

I thank God for the vision and the words to speak my truth. This book is dedicated to my late grandmother Julia May Hill who always poured into me through her words. To my mother Eunice Lorraine Powell for life itself. To my two sisters Camella and Jeanine who know and have lived the same story of sacrifice and perseverance. To my boys Christopher and Isaiah who taught me the true meaning of unconditional love and gave me the right to hold my greatest title ever of Mom. To my cousin Anngenette who never forgot my sisters and I, even when it seems as if everyone else did. To my Antie who encouraged me to live life on my terms. To the Army who made my dreams a reality. To all my family and friends who have always believed in me, even when I didn't believe in myself.

Every new day is an opportunity to be better than you were the day before. There are lessons hidden in yesterday, but you must be intentional to receive them.

—Jessica N. Waller

Introduction

As I sat in the room with tears in my eyes, I looked down at my son and knew I had to leave. If I stayed in this situation, the biggest lesson I would give him was that it was okay to physically and verbally abuse the ones you say you love. I brought all the books about domestic violence and hid them under the bathroom sink in the hopes that he my abuser would not find them. I was at the lowest point in my life. I was 20 years old with a newborn baby and couldn't see pass each day. This time he attacked me because he didn't like the tone I used. This time he struck me while I had our son in my arms. In an attempt to defend myself, I grabbed his white t-shirt, which ended up ripping at the collar. This enraged him even more, and he continued to attack me. He then demanded two dollars to replace the shirt that I ripped while he attacked me. I gave him the two dollars, and he left.

When he left, I knew what I had to do. I grabbed everything that my son would need and a few essential items for myself. I called my best friend's mother, who picked me up to take me to the homeless shelter emergency assistance unit. I had never been so afraid and uncertain in my life. The brutal attacks while I was pregnant, the mind games, the threat of home-made abortions with a metal hanger, and the constant reminder that I did not have anyone to defend me had finally worn me down. Who would protect Jessica? Who could I tell? I pretended I was okay with everyone, but I wasn't okay. I was scared. I had been renting a room that cost eighty dollars a week, and I made one hundred and twenty a week at my job. Nothing was left when I got a metro card and food for the week. Despite this, I was still attending school full-time, and I was exhausted. I did not end up in labor on the train to work the day my son was born because my contractions started at six a.m., and I got on the train around seven a.m. I worked until the last day of my pregnancy and returned to work one week after having my son. I couldn't afford to stay home. Who would pay the bills?

This was my complete introduction to adulthood, motherhood, and love, all wrapped up in one. So many days, I wondered if I had listened to what my grandmother said would things be different? If only I had heeded her advice. There were so many nuggets for everyday living within her words. So much heartache that I could've avoided if only I had listened. My grandmother was a critical and constant part of my life from age seven to thirty-seven. She was always there, always offering words of encouragement. Sometimes her words didn't always feel like encouragement because they were so harsh, but they were. Her words stuck with me throughout life. I understood that while her tone was rough, she meant well. As children, we don't always want to hear it; however, those words will ring loud and clear in our silent moments. It will all make sense once you're in a place to receive the message.

This book highlights some of the sayings my grandmother always told me growing up. Although she is no longer here, her words still have much meaning and applicability to my everyday life. At the age of nine, I told my grandmother I would publish my first book by thirty. At 21, I let her read the first chapter of a book I had written, and she told me I needed to finish it. Over the years, she would ask me what was going on with my book. She always reminded me I needed to finish what I had started. The completion of that book never happened, and I still have the hundred-something typed pages in my home. However, while this is not the book that she expected, this book is a labor of love for her. How befitting that my first book will be focused on her words that have always been a lighthouse to my life.

Just Keep Living

*L*iving is a choice. Every day without much thought, we choose to keep living. One of the things my grandmother used to say to me whenever I was confused or perplexed by something was, "Just keep living." I would get frustrated by this response as I needed help understanding the meaning behind this. I would think to myself, I don't have a choice in living; now I know I always did. Living is the easy part; how you live is where it gets complicated. As I grew older, I fully understood what she truly meant. Life has a way of teaching us some lessons without intentionally learning them.

At the age of 19, I was young and full of zeal. I entered a relationship with my eyes wide open, or should I say wired shut. I led with my heart, and although all the signs were there and red flags existed, I decided to ignore them. I was in love, and no one could tell me anything, especially not the older folks. What did they know? Yes, he had a criminal record and was recently released from prison. He was arrested at 16 and charged with armed robbery. He was released after serving three years. So many people judged his situation, but who was I to judge? His life mirrored my father, whom I loved dearly. Judge not lest we be judged, isn't that what the good book says? Of course, we can manipulate scripture to work for our good as needed, and that's exactly what I did. But there is judging, and then there is just common sense.

I continued to move forward in this relationship, and eventually, at the age of 19, I found myself pregnant and in a physically and emotionally abusive relationship. Earlier I mentioned his incarceration, not as a red flag to me, but it was what others perceived as a disqualifier. Let me be clear that incarceration alone is not a precursor to someone being physically abusive. The fact that he was aggressive in his actions and wanted to control what began as little things grew substantially over the months that followed. I mistakenly believed that popping up where I was or asking me why I had to go out with my friends was out of love and adoration. When he got angry when I spoke to other males, that was because he loved me and wanted me all to himself. Growing up with a father who was present in waves due to spending the majority of his life in and out of prison, I was happy to receive attention and what I perceived as love from a man. I felt like judging him for his time in prison was like I was judging my father. I believed I could change him and give him a chance that society did not often give our young black men following incarceration.

I had known my child's father since I was seven years old. His mother used to babysit me; we practically grew up together. He had a mean streak as a child and often picked on my sister and me. But isn't that what most boys do at that age? As teenagers, he wasn't around much, but our relationship was cordial. Later, at sixteen he got into some trouble and was locked up. While in prison, we became pen pals, and the correspondence was always friendly. When he returned from prison, I offered to take him to dinner as a welcome home, and things grew from there. By the following year, I was pregnant with my son and being abused by someone who said they loved me.

Life quickly taught me that everyone is not worth saving and some people must want the change for themselves. Sometimes, you can want something for someone more than they want it for themselves. If this is the case, your efforts are futile, and you will end up exhausting yourself. You may even push that person to the point of resentment. Your push can make them feel you need more than where they are heading. I thought I could change my son's father. I could encourage him to go to school and get a job. I thought our son would be enough to change him. Maybe after our son, he would stop physically abusing me. This never happened; people change only when they are ready. If you keep living, life will continually teach you lessons. Some lessons we learn the hard way. Those hard lessons are the most memorable. You can be told the fire is hot, but nothing like the sizzle of your skin to ensure you keep the appropriate distance and give fire the respect it deserves. He was the fire, and that relationship was the sizzle. Going forward, I was very cognizant of who I got romantically involved with.

In Job 14:7 the Bible tells us, "There is hope for a tree when it is cut down, that it will sprout again, and its shoots will not fail." What this means is even when things are cut down, even when life throws you a curve ball or things don't work out there is value there. While I wish I did not experience a physically abusive relationship, teenage pregnancy, or homelessness, there were valuable lessons embedded within that contributed to the person I am today. Being in an abusive relationship taught me early in life to recognize signs. I learned to take the time to understand what true love looks like and what it should feel like. Being a young parent taught me what unconditional love felt like and how to give it to someone else. My son motivated me to accomplish everything I wanted before I became pregnant. I thought they were no longer attainable once I was pregnant, but I proved myself wrong. Sometimes your thoughts are your biggest obstacle. I had to get over disappointing myself. Living in a homeless shelter for victims of domestic violence gave me the courage to push forward and later minister through my testimony to others. My story encouraged others that where they started does not and will not determine where they end.

I went through shame, guilt, self-blame, and a gamut of emotions while overcoming many obstacles.

When I had to take a semester off from college while I was in the shelter, I believed it was over for me. I believed life was over when the pregnancy test showed positive at 19. When he hit me for the first time while pregnant and threatened to give me an at-home abortion, I believed life was over. BUT GOD... had bigger plans for my life. God had given me free choice, and I made some poor decisions. However, he never left my side. I was always his daughter, and he was always my heavenly father. The fatherly love I was looking for in a mate was there all along through God. I was young and didn't understand God's love at the time. I thought what I was going through resulted from not obeying God's word. But my God does not work like that; he forgives and looks at the heart. There was hope when my tree was cut down, and I did sprout again. It took some time, but what grew out of that was a woman of faith, strength, and a loving mother to two handsome young men.

I pushed through college with my youngest son because I knew it would encourage him to do the same if I completed my degree. In 2004 I completed my Bachelor of Arts in public administration. In 2009 I completed my Master of Science in management with a concentration in public relations. The biggest victory was not my completion of those degrees but my son's completion of his Bachelor of Science in health care administration in 2022. The young boy that I fled his father's grasp for a better life for him made it! The young boy I sat in a homeless shelter with while crying to sleep made something out of himself. He broke the generational curse of incarceration!

Life requires you to keep living, most importantly, to live intentionally. It wasn't one failed abusive relationship, and I was set straight. However, going forward, I looked for certain signs and left abruptly if there was an inkling you might have a problem with your hands. There were multiple heartbreaks, but none were as abusive as the first one. I learned the lesson about abuse quickly. I was determined not to live in fear again. As we say in the Army, "One shot, one kill." it took one time for me to get the message.

However, all was not peaches and cream moving forward. You don't get the healing if you don't do the work. As a result of not receiving the healing I needed following that relationship, I became the aggressor. I lacked the emotional maturity to deal with conflict in my next relationship. I wasn't abusing him; however, after being in a previous situation where arguments led to physical attacks, I attacked before he could. If things appeared to be heading in that direction, I would lash out before he could because that's where this is leading, right? The wrong answer, I had conditioned myself to believe that conflict led to physical attacks, and I was not going to be the punching bag. I did not do the required work after that relationship. I went to the next relationship with my baggage. Eventually, that relationship failed, and I moved on with life, never unpacking. So now the bag was full of trauma, abuse, hurt, mistrust, and self-esteem issues.

Through it all life continued to life, and I was cut down and regrown. However, as I was cut down, I always remained confident in God's word that I would sprout again, and I did. But most importantly, as grandma said, I had to keep living. Life's lessons will be revealed through living, but we must open our hearts and ears to receive.

Every Monkey Knows
What Tree to Climb

I bet you're laughing at this title, and it seems so random. However, if you stick with me, I promise it will make sense. Some people take on tasks only if they are 100% certain they can accomplish them. Every monkey knows what tree to climb is something my grandmother would always say to me, and I would look at her with a slight smile or annoyance. It was her way of saying someone was getting over because they knew they could. That's me breaking it down in the simplest of terms. She often said this when my kids manipulated me to get something they wanted. Primarily it would be "that little one" as she affectionately referred to my youngest son, amongst other nicknames. He had a way of getting what he wanted out of me. She also said this when she became aware of the physical abuse I suffered at the hands of my son's father. She believed he treated me this way because he knew he could get away with it. I didn't have my father or any males around that could stand in the gap and protect me. He knew this and took full advantage of it.

After my grandmother's passing in 2017, I sought and found a deeper understanding of everything she said. Sometimes as I went down memory lane, I would laugh, and other times I would have these eureka moments thinking I've finally got it! While every monkey knows what trees to climb, within the context she used, this always referred to individuals being manipulated; I've now attached this to a very different meaning. This new meaning is from a more positive and biblical perspective. In all honesty, my thought process about something I've heard my entire life changed during the writing of this book. The phrase made me think about your true potential or the things you pursue. If we only climb the easy trees or attempt to do the things we know we can accomplish, we are never pushing ourselves to the greatness that God has for all of us.

Some of us do not fully realize the greatness we harness; this is evident through the fact that we only climb the trees we can successfully reach the top without issue. Imagine if we took a chance on something that was not guaranteed, but we followed our hearts instead. God did not give us a spirit of fear but of power and of love and of instruction (2 Timothy 1:7). I recently had a conversation with my 15-year-old about his future career endeavors and what he ultimately wants out of life. First, I did not realize that he spent so much time worrying about the future. I thought to myself zeesh, enjoy life, but I also applauded him for taking a very proactive stance in his future. He expressed wanting to be a veterinarian but was discouraged by the required years of schooling. I encouraged him and told him I would support him every step of the way if this were something he truly wanted. He has always been very passionate about animals. From an early age gravitated toward any creepy, crawly, furry thing he could find. I am envious of people who find their passion early in life. I am searching for my passion as I push toward retirement in my first career. After 25 years in the military, my passion has become the military. After adulting for so long, I lost that passion and stopped dreaming. My thoughts for life after retirement from the army are who will pay me well to do something that I am knowledgeable and capable of executing with high proficiency. Sounds lame, but that's all I've got now, no big grandiose dreams.

Regarding my son, there were some things I grew to an understanding of over the years regarding parenting. As a parent, I have realized that we must be intentional with how we pour into our children. Our words and tone matter when we speak to our children. I remember working with someone who told me he and his wife would tell their children how great they were every night. They would whisper words of affirmation to them as they slept. I thought this was amazing. It reminded me that we harness so much power through our words. We all possess the ability to change a situation just by the words that we speak over it. There is so much benefit to opening your mouth and saying to yourself the things you need to hear. Providing yourself with words of affirmation is a game changer. Words of affirmation are a powerful tool for self-development and spiritual alignment. If we continuously tell ourselves certain things, we will eventually believe them. That goes for negativity and positivity. Be careful of the words you speak over your own life and those around you. When you begin to believe those words, they will manifest in your actions and how you live your life.

When encountering life issues, be intentional with how you frame the problem. How you present the problem to yourself can ultimately determine your willingness to engage and overcome it. How we frame a problem in our minds determines how we tackle it. Are we looking at the problem as something almost impossible to solve, or are we looking at it as a challenge that you will be the first to conquer? While my son has barely begun his path to becoming a veterinarian, he already views it as too many years of schooling; essentially, he's already removed himself from the race with this thought process. He is not viewing the tree as climbable (is that a word? if not, we're still going to roll with it). We can psych ourselves out of a winning and, ultimately victory through our thought process.

Once we have framed something in our minds, the next step is our willingness to engage. Are you only engaging in the things that you are positive you can accomplish? Are you climbing only the trees you know can reach the top? What opportunities have you missed out on because you remained where you were comfortable and lacked the desire to take a chance? While being comfortable is great, there are times when being too comfortable can be detrimental to success. In these situations, we seize to grow. Sometimes growth comes from being uncomfortable. Comfort can kill relationships; in the season of comfort, you may put forth less effort. When I reference relationships, I am not only referencing relationships between a man and a woman. You can be comfortable in your relationship with friends, putting forth minimal effort to develop and nurture the development of the friendship. There is workplace comfortability where you have remained at the same level with no career progression because you are comfortable where you are. Life is easier there, but you're not living in the fullness you are destined for. Many of us are comfortable in our relationship with God. Worship becomes routine and mundane; your heart is no longer in it. There is no spiritual growth when we become too comfortable with our interactions with God.

When we become comfortable, we no longer tap into our true potential, and thus we cannot grow. Life is an opportunity for continual development and discovery. I seek opportunities to grow if I find myself stagnant in an area for too long. Now, let me be clear there are times in our life when you must "peace be still" to hear God. God's voice becomes so clear to me in the stillness of those moments. I must remind myself to sit down and take a tactical pause to gather my thoughts and figure out life. I use the word tactical because of my military background and secondly because you are strategizing even in taking that pause. Sometimes I sit back and look at the things I have planned and become overwhelmed, thinking to myself, what did you think when you planned all of this? This is not where I seek anyone reading this book to be. Pace yourself and do not overextend yourself in the name of progressing to the point that you are stretched thin. This can cause additional stress, which could ultimately lead to health issues. Primarily for me, it was anxiety and high blood pressure. However, I seek to always be in forward motion but remember to take breaks, aka tactical pauses.

Even during your breaks, you can plan ahead but give yourself time to replenish.

The failure to take breaks as needed has carried over into other areas of my life. As I reflect on my relationships, it becomes clear that I never took the breaks to refocus on myself. I moved from one relationship to the next. When you do this, you bring everything with you and drag it into your next relationship, which can be toxic. You will eventually get to the point where it becomes too much because you never offloaded anything. As Erykah Badu titled it you are the "Bag Lady". Even worse, your body has become so acclimated to the weight you've been carrying for years that it won't know how to respond when you release the weight. This is the danger zone where I found myself when I finally took a break. I was so used to carrying around all the hurt, anger, pain, fear, and disappointment that it had become normal. These emotions were ME. When I let go of these things, my body was confused. It was as if my body went into shock, and now new emotions came into play in the form of anxiety. I couldn't wrap my mind around this because, for once in my life, I no longer had the external stressors, and anxiety crept in.

However, the point remains that in pursuing greatness, take a break for rest, recover, and re-strategize.

Back to the original point before I got sidetracked with the importance of taking a break when you feel overwhelmed, we mustn't become too settled and comfortable to the point where we are not growing in our spiritual journey, relationships, and career. Breaks are great, and those breaks create opportunities for you to reflect and absorb the world around you. With that being said, always push yourself to be the greatest version of you. In doing so, you will reach your maximum potential. Don't only climb the trees you know you can reach the top. Where is the challenge in that? Be like the monkey that knows which trees to climb but don't forget to take some risks on the ones that appear uncertain. If you don't take risks, you are limiting yourself. In life, sometimes even the monkey miscalculates the enormity of the tree and its branches, he may fall, but he still survives. Please do not limit yourself by always playing it safe. Take the hard right and embark upon the uncertain journey. Through this perseverance and tough encounters, you reach your maximum potential. Climb the tree!

The Grass Always Looks Greener on the Other Side

The grass always looks greener on the other side, but if you water your grass, it will be just as green was something my grandma used to say when I longed for something else or coveted what someone else had. Whether you realize it or not, you may have coveted what others have at some point in your life. Today, with the boom of social media, many of us find ourselves looking at other lives and wanting what they have. Not wanting the lives they have built for themselves but perhaps wanting the associated perceived "happiness". Maybe, you think, when will I find that type of love? When will I purchase my first home, complete a degree, land my dream job, get the promotion, travel, or whatever else piques your interest. If you're like me, the target is fleeting as you add new endeavors to your bucket list.

I recently traveled to Vermont to see firsthand the coveted fall foliage. This experience was a bucket list item I added to my ever-growing list; I've always loved the fall. My grandmother and I would drive down the road and marvel at the hand of God during the fall season. She would point out a tree with orange, red, or burgundy hues, and I would look on in awe. When I arrived in Vermont, the fall foliage was everything I imagined. As I reflected on life, I appreciated the beauty of the trees, but I also fully embraced the fullness of where I was in life. On the way up, my children teased that driving to see the fall foliage was not something "we" engaged in. I realized then that sometimes life and the cards you are dealt do not offer you the time to pause and just enjoy and appreciate life.

As a single mother, a survivor of a domestic violence relationship, and homelessness, my earlier years did not give way to stopping and watching the trees. I was in survival mode, and there was no stopping allowed. While my children played along and began enjoying nature, I was at complete peace because this moment meant much more to me. This moment was freedom. This moment signified something much more profound. I was at a point where I could finally stop and smell the roses, and it did not smell like boo-boo (yup, kind of lame). Going back to my original points, God never gave me a heart of jealousy. However, I had moments of wanting the life others freely enjoyed. As I grew within myself, I celebrated other people's successes fully and wholeheartedly. Not feeling a tinge of jealousy or hate toward their accomplishments. When I think I lack in any area, I always remember to pour into myself and remain thankful for where I am in my present life. I am reminded to thank God for where he will eventually lead me. I thank him before I take my first step in that direction.

After driving to Vermont, I returned home and had this aha moment while washing the dishes. I looked out the window and saw the most beautiful tree. I thought to myself here it is that I went all the way to Vermont and failed to recognize the beauty right in front of me. Sometimes, we fail to acknowledge what we have when we focus on what others may have. We are constantly inundated with images of social statuses and materialistic items via social media. We see a photo of a happy couple and may immediately feel like they have something we want. We fail to realize that the photo depicts a second, a moment in time. We may be coveting something that is not even real. We don't see the whole story. We simply see a picture. Some of my best family photos were taken after yelling at everyone to take them. They were miserable and saying, "Not another photo." You saw a happy family, but did you know the struggle before? When we begin to feel that we are not successful in our own right or want what others have, we can look to scripture for guidance. Deuteronomy 8:18 tells us to remember the Lord our God, he is the one who gives you power to be successful. Remembering God and standing fast on his word removes the spirit of jealousy or a covetous heart. We know that all good things come from him, including our success. Through this remembrance, we can appreciate where we are and remember, as my grandmother used to say, "If you water your own grass, it will be just as green." Pour into yourself and avoid focusing on what others may have. Focusing on others can plant the seed of jealousy, anger, and depression.

Time and Tide
Wait for No One

Time is a gift from God. It is a valuable resource that, once it's been expended, we can never replace it. Unfortunately, most of us don't realize the importance of time until it has already passed. Time will never cease to move forward, and the tide will always roll in. The tides may be high or low, but they will continuously roll. Tides reflect the ups and downs that life will bring. When the tide is high, we enjoy everything life has to offer and yield the results of our work. On the other hand, the low tide represents the points in our lives when we are presented with adversity. It is with certainty that we know we will experience both throughout our lives. As the years go by, we suddenly find ourselves reflecting on the time loss. We begin thinking about what we could've done with that time. Over the years, I've given my time to people, issues, and circumstances that did not deserve a millisecond of it. Why do we give time to circumstances or things that do not deserve it? I argue that it is because we do not use prudence in a lot of our decision making thus leading to expended time without the desired results. We must use prudence in all situations, particularly with how we spend our time. Prudence allows us to exercise caution against danger or risks. In effectively using prudence, we can make better use of our time.

Every year I am flabbergasted by how fast time goes by. The new year rolls in; two seconds later it is spring; a minute later summer, and before you know it, you are planning Thanksgiving dinner and Christmas shopping. The time is exponentially faster when you have a family to provide for and a career to manage. If we are not intentional with our time, we may realize that we've accomplished very little and wasted days, months, or even years of our lives. During a heated discussion with a guy I was dating, I blurted out, "Why did you waste my time?' His response was, "Waste your time!! I can't waste your time." I thought for a second and realized he was 100% right. I gave him my time; it was my time to give. I gave it freely and was not held hostage against my will. As his words resonated with me, I thought about how much time I had given to other people.

I remember feeling as if I had wasted so much time in my life. So many times, I felt as if I was behind the power curve and playing catch up to my peers who did not have children or made some of the terrible decisions I had. It was vital for me to realize that there was no established timeline to greatness. The timelines were the ones I created and imposed upon myself. Some people go to college immediately following high school and graduate in four years. Others take a semester off and finish a little later. Some never go to college and have much success being an entrepreneur or something else. This does not make anyone more accomplished than the other. I had to learn this throughout my life. When I compared myself to others, I began to feel less valuable. Through this comparison, I focused my efforts more on finishing because someone else had done it rather than getting the full benefit and wholeheartedly embracing the process. The process is just as if not more important than the results.

In my forties, I had given at least half of my life to failed relationships. I use failed with some hesitation as I believe there is a lesson in everything. However, they failed because they didn't last or end up in marriage as we think relationships should unless you're dating for fun. Hindsight, it would've been more productive to use that time I spent in multiple relationships to understand myself better and engage in some much-needed healing. Failure to do so led me to engage in a reoccurring cycle of bad habits. I was self-sabotaging situations by not using my time in between relationships to do the work that was required of me. During this time, I failed to listen to the voice of God and was following my own will.

In the past, I have had difficulty differentiating between God's will and my own will. Honestly, this is still a struggle, but I'm improving. Previously, before opening my heart, eyes, and ears, I ran interference with God's plan through my strong will and personal desires. My will did not allow me to see what God's intentions for me were at the time. While avoiding the obvious hazards, I was not paying close attention to things that could present a real danger. Those things ultimately consumed time that I didn't always have to give. Time spent trying to fix what was damaged.

Chapter three of Ecclesiastes talks about time in depth. There is a time for everything and a season for every activity under the heavens. In this Bible chapter, I am reminded that everything is preordained and happens when it is supposed to. It tells us there is a time to be born and die, a time to plant and uproot. Nothing in life is by happenstance.

There is a time for everything. In knowing this it is essential to living that you know the season in which you are operating in your life. Is this the time to lay down roots, or is it the time to move? What time in your life is this? Aligning your use of time with the season you are operating in is crucial to becoming good stewards of our time. In the same chapter of Ecclesiastes, we are told there is a time to be silent and a time to speak. Sometimes in our lives, your silence is more powerful than your speech. Know when to speak and when to speak through your silence. Once words leave your mouth, you cannot rescind them. The effects of your words linger long after you've said them. I remember words spoken to me as young as four. Hurtful words especially last a lot longer in our memories.

We are also told in Ecclesiastes that there is a time to tear and mend. Sometimes we must break away from circumstances that are no longer productive to who we are. These situations may pull us away from the covering of God. Perhaps, these situations keep us angry, or we focus so much on our emotions over it that we begin to rob God of his time. The Bible also tells us there is a time to mend. A time to restore those relationships and things that were once destroyed. Have you ever walked away from a situation and something within you never felt quite settled about it. You tore away from the situation, but it never felt right in your spirit. Or it did feel right at the time, but you still revisit that situation mentally years later. You contemplate the different ways you could have handled things. It may be time to revisit and reconcile. It is time to have a difficult conversation with the person and mend things.

Years after the physical abuse from my son's father, he called me to apologize. I had already let go of things years prior, but he had not. He apologized profusely. I accepted his apology and cut the conversation short. I did not want to revisit that part of my life. I had closed the chapter and felt it was unnecessary to have the conversation. I later learned the door was closed, but behind it, the issues remained. I needed to deal with the abuse directly instead of shutting it out. In any event, my son's father was mending something he had torn down. That apology was closure for him. I took no issue with this. I understood for whatever season of his life he was in; he needed this.

Time should never be taken for granted. Through God's word, we know there is a time for everything we go through. Certain situations can block us from our blessings and serve as a roadblock or detour to the life God has prepared for us. If you encounter a roadblock or a detour, what does that do to your travel plans? It delays you from arriving at the destination at the prescribed time. Keep in mind that even when our plans are delayed that does not mean they are denied. We can still access God's blessing and tap into our full potential; however, it may take a little longer.

Being cognizant and respectful of time has groomed me to be in tune with where I invest my energy. Being sensitive to time has allowed me to be more intentional with my thoughts. Our thoughts ultimately lead our actions. We have a thought, and that thought later becomes an action. If I am focusing my thoughts on where others are in life, this is wasted time, yielding little results. However, if I focus on the things I want for myself and the greatness that God has destined for me, my actions will be more fruitful. Additionally, it is essential that in making good use of our time, we focus on the right things. We make the most of our time by being intentional with our thoughts and our actions. We must take an active stance in all areas of our lives. If we are not intentional, we allow others to slip in and control the narrative of our life.

The devil has mastered the art of finding a way in when we are taking a laissez-faire approach to our lives. The devil seeks to destroy, conquer, and control. That is why it is imperative to know the voice of God and have a relationship with him. It is important to be active in our lives by taking control of our time. This sounds simple right? How can we not be active in our own lives? Think back to how many times you've been on cruise control passively going through life. You arrive at a destination and question how you got there. I look back on segments of my life that are now a blur; I was going through the motions. I was in the driver's seat, but mentally I was in the passenger seat, distracted by life. Allowing life to dictate the next stop, rather than taking control of the route to the next destination. The devil takes joy when we are on cruise control because, ultimately, we are making him the driver. The devil's destination is not in alignment with where God wants us to go, although he may attempt to mask parts of the journey to appear that way. My grandmother's statement of time and tide waiting for no one emphasized realizing that life will continue to move forward. How we manage our time and mitigate the highs and lows is essential.

Your Family is Wished Upon You

We don't get to choose the family that we are born into. Although, I am sure many of us wish this were an option. Oh, the families we would choose, only to be later disappointed that the family you thought was ideal was just as cracked up as yours…NO BACKSIES!! I came into this world as a twin, following my fraternal twin sister by precisely one minute. I was born to a mother and father who both suffered from addiction. While I wouldn't change my family, I would definitely change the circumstances under which I was born. The old lady used to always say your family is wished upon you, but if you get yourself a few good friends in life, you won't know the difference between that and family. What she wanted us to understand is that you don't get to choose the family you are born with, but you do choose your friends. In doing so, be sure to choose your friends wisely.

Family is a huge part of my life; I have a huge family, but I don't connect with many of them outside of Facebook. I love the idea of family, but as everyone grew older, there was a huge disconnect. No disagreements just family grew apart. The days of the family living within blocks of one another changed as people moved to other areas for better opportunities amongst other things. For my immediate family of aunts and uncles' which were my mother siblings, their battles with addiction and disease took three of the six at an early age. They all passed away in their twenties. One of them was my mother, who passed away at 29 leaving my two sisters and me.

In my early years, it seemed like everyone came to my mother's house every Friday to hang out and get high. I remember my cousins, aunts, and uncles at the house and everyone having a good time. Music playing, dancing, story-telling (My uncle Maine was the best at this), and the kids begging the adults to go to the store and get us candy. Once my mother passed away, our life came to an abrupt halt. My sisters and I went to live with my grandmother. There was three of us my twin and my oldest sister. She was older than us by four years, which back then seemed like so much. She was the second in charge after my mother and later grandmother.

After her diagnosis, my mother became terminally ill. My mother was in the hospital for two years, and I remember very few of those same family members at the house every week coming to visit her in the hospital. Additionally, the family I had grown to know who visited my mother's house every week disappeared; we no longer saw them except for some holidays. It felt like not only did we lose my mother, but we also lost an entire family. It was just the three of us and my grandmother now. I will say one of my cousins who was ten years our senior never forgot about us. She always visited and would come to get us for the weekend. I am forever grateful for her sacrifice. While I loved being with my grandmother, it was great to be around some youthful energy when she came to get us. The fact that we no longer saw family bothered my twin and me. It made matters worse that my older sister left home abruptly a few years later. She connected us to the life we knew before and was like a second mother to us. When she left my sister and I were devastated. I remember my twin sister and I talking to my grandmother about family and feeling like everyone abandoned us. That is when my grandmother told us that your family was wished upon you but your friends you chose. She encouraged us to choose our friends wisely; if we did this, we would not know the difference between that and family.

The ability to choose who we surround ourselves with is a blessing and a task not to be taken lightly. Over the years, I have been very intentional with the people I choose to have in my life. There may be a point in my life when my family is unavailable. During those times, the ones I have chosen to be a part of my life will be there to support me. Being a single mom in the military it is vital to establish a support system. This support system is comprised of family, friends, and professional childcare. As a soldier, there were times when I had to work weekends or travel last minute in support of a mission. It was my friends who stepped up to the plate and held things down for me while I was away. I would not be where I am in my career without this network of friends. My neighbor, who later became family, would pick the kids up when I worked late or watch them while I traveled. I will never forget her support throughout the years. Let's be clear I don't select friends based on who will be available when no one else is, but I select like-minded individuals that understand the value of friendship.

Proverbs 18:24 states that one who has unreliable friends soon comes to ruin, but there is a friend who sticks closer than a brother. I love this verse for multiple reasons. It emphasizes the impact of not having reliable friends you can depend on. Ruin is a strong word. I wondered why this word was chosen. The word ruin refers to something being destroyed or disintegrated. Being in the wrong company could ultimately lead to your demise. This word emphasizes how detrimental it is not to surround yourself with reliable friends. However, the same verse offers us solace in knowing that even if you have unreliable friends, God is rock solid. God is the ultimate friend and family member who will always be there.

We all need a strong support system, whether that is your church family, biological family, or hand-picked family. It is also vital to note that you should be the friend you want. A friendship must be balanced. It cannot be a relationship comprised of a taker and a giver. I am not encouraging only selecting friends that you see a benefit in. I suggest that you are intentional with the selection of the people that you will later call friends.

Everyone is not your friend, and that is okay. You will not be everyone's friend, which is also okay. You don't need an entourage of people in your life. You simply need the ones who will be there when the rubber hits the road. You also need those who can enjoy life with you because life is good. In my grandmother's words, your family is wished upon you, but you choose your friends. If you choose your friends well, you won't know the difference between that and family. Choose them wisely!

When you're in a
Hole Quit Digging

I t may be best to be still in the moment and re-group when you find yourself amid troubling times. My grandmother would stop me midsentence when she presumed I was lying or going too far with my antics. With a stern parental look she mastered, my grandmother would look me in the face and say when you're in a hole, quit digging. I knew immediately it was a good idea to stop and rethink how far I wanted to go with whatever story I was telling. The thought process behind her statement was things could only get worse if you continued along the path you were going. As a parent, I find myself uttering those exact words to my children when they have gone too far with just about anything. They stopped as I did some many years earlier when those words were spoken to me. However, having more boldness than I clearly had growing up, they will typically respond with, "I'm not lying." In return, I will shoot them a glance, signaling I'm serious and this is not up for debate or watch your tone of voice.

As an adult, I can't say I have mastered the art of quitting when I'm in too deep. However, I have become more in tune with my body and external factors to know when things are going too far. These days external cues to quit are not after I have spoken a lie, there are in reference to my mental or physical state. These cues tell me to take a break. I have a habit of pushing myself to the limit and not realizing that I have overcommitted myself to a multitude of activities. During my conversations with other people, they would respond with, "wow, that's a lot." it is only then that I began to think that perhaps I have obligated myself to more than I can handle. Recently, I decided to take a pause and slow down a bit. I opened my schedule and became still for a while. What happened next threw me for a loop. I experienced an influx of emotions. I found myself thinking about my past and some of the low points throughout my life. Things began to come to the surface that I had not considered in years. I began to question what was going on with me and why my energy was so low. I felt anxious and suffered from panic attacks. I decided to speak with a counselor. The sessions were eye-opening and revealed a lot that I had not considered.

From an early age, I dealt with extreme trauma. When I was nine, my mother passed away after a two-year battle with AIDS. It was devastating to watch my mother deteriorate and know eventually; she would succumb to her illness. It was a constant question of when she would pass away, not if. After every visit, I wondered if this would be the last time I would see her. My sisters and I watched bed after bed become empty as other patients died when we visited her in the AIDS ward. Some of the patients that passed were people we befriended during our visits. One week they would be walking around and talking with us. The next week bedridden, and eventually, they would be gone. Being diagnosed was a death sentence. In the 1980s individuals with AIDS were treated with what I imagine to be similar to attitudes and behaviors towards individuals with leprosy in the bible. This was the earliest onset of trauma for me. The coping mechanisms I developed were through learned and taught behavior.

After my mother passed, my grandmother was intentional about keeping us busy. We were in every activity that you could imagine. This gave us very little time to remain focused on the trauma. This way of coping worked. However, it taught me a lack of vulnerability to my emotions and the necessity to push forward regardless of the circumstances. This works until you stop and sit still, which happened in my 40's. I had not dealt with earlier trauma, and now coupled with the loss of my grandmother a few years prior, things were compiled, and I foolishly made the mistake of sitting still. I use the words foolishly and mistake very loosely, as it became clear through counseling that I needed to take a break. According to the counselor, I was in flight or fight mode most of my life. I was in survival mode as a single mother, a victim of abuse, homelessness, and loss. In this mode, my body became comfortable dealing with trauma and the associated heightened emotions. However, once life settled and I no longer had the stress of all these things, my body could begin to process everything. The processing of the ALL was a lot and brought on a different type of heightened emotional response and increased anxiety. She explained this much more eloquently than I did, but this is the gist of what I got from it. It can become challenging to understand what is happening if you are constantly in motion. STOP,,, that's what I had to do; I had to finally take the time to process my life and understand what I went through. Even the Lord took a break when he created the heavens and the earth.

I realized there were points in my life where I blamed myself for what happened to me. If I had not left the hospital during that last visit with my mother, she would have lived just a little longer, although her death was inevitable. If I had done something differently on that last day at my grandmother's house before she fell and was in a coma for three months before eventually passing, I wholeheartedly believed she would still be here. I didn't realize I was carrying around that guilt since I stayed in constant motion. It made matters worse when I was discussing with my children what was one thing they would change if they could. My youngest, who had no ill intention when he said it uttered what I had been feeling for three years. "I wished you would've stayed with grandma at her house that day." I was floored but played it off. He said it so casually and matter-of-factly as he gazed out the car window. Wow, someone else felt what I had been thinking and beating myself up about. I pushed the emotions to the back of my mind and busied myself with life. I also blamed myself for being in an abusive relationship. The self-blame game is dangerous. Why did I not listen to those who told me dating him was a bad idea? I had to learn that I couldn't make someone hit me, even if I asked for it. The abuser always possesses free will and choice for their actions.

Some of these lessons seem so simple. These lessons are easy to utter to others as you give a pep talk or encouragement. However, these same lessons are much harder to convince yourself of being true. That is where I struggled. I had difficulty convincing myself that I held no responsibility for some of the things that happened to me. Some of us are the best advice givers but are the worst receivers of advice. I am most certainly guilty of this. I could tell you precisely what you should do from beginning to end but not do the same for myself. I could tell you how beautiful you were and give you the pep talk of your life but not pour into myself the same way. Do therapists struggle with this? When I took that break, I immediately sought counseling when things felt weird, for lack of a better term.

In taking a break and seeking counseling when my emotions began to spiral, I provided myself with much-needed self-care. Self-care is one of the most essential forms of care for you and those around you. I know we hear this all the time, but you cannot pour from an empty cup. When I am depleted, and in a hole, I can no longer be 100% as a mom, a friend, a Soldier, or anything else I am focused on. I was angry when I was depleted and dealing with my own emotional turmoil. My tolerance was low, and I was doing a lot of yelling. Moreso than my usual mom yelling. I needed to realize where I was and stop digging deeper into an emotional rut. I sat still and listened to the world around me and what God wanted me to hear.

In the bible, God spoke to many of his followers in their moments of solitude. When you are alone, I believe the silence allows us to hear the voice of God. When referring to biblical scripture, most people went to the desert or the mountains to be alone, and it was where they heard the voice of God. In comparison, this represents a moment of stillness and solitude…a break. Although my grandmother used the saying when you're in a hole, quit digging as a cue to stop me from lying or further getting into trouble, there were so many areas of applicability as I thought of her words. When I found myself at an emotional low, I had to quit before I was at the point of no return. I have to quit when I am overwhelmed with work/life balance. Most importantly, it is in those moments of quitting that I receive my breakthrough. Through this breakthrough, I am replenished enough to dig myself out versus deeper. Tell yourself sometimes it's okay to quit!

Show Me Your Company and I Will Tell You Who You Are

*W*ho's your favorite five or Fav 5 as T-Mobile used to say. Your Fav 5 with T-Mobile cellular plan were those five people you could call without being charged your daytime minutes. These younger folks do not know anything about daytime minutes. They don't know the struggle of waiting until nine at night to make calls without going over your plan. But I digress; let me get back on track. Who are the people that you stay connected to? Who are the ones that pour into you when you are depleted? The answer to this question is essential to understanding some things about yourself. The Bible tells us in Matthew 7:15-20 that we can tell a tree by the type of fruit it produces. "Wherefore by their fruits, ye shall know them." Fruits represent a myriad of things to me. Fruits are a representation of me and the things I surround myself with. My children are my fruit; their behavior in my absence represents me. My friends are also my fruit; they do not belong to me but who I surround myself with says a lot about me. Thus, show me your company, and I will tell you who you are.

If you spend a great deal of time with a group of people, their attributes will eventually rub off on you. If your friends cuss a lot, it won't be long before you have a potty mouth. If your friends are engaged in extramarital affairs, I'm not saying you will engage; however, it could lower your moral standard by consistently being around the behavior. The more it's around you, the fewer issues you may have with it. Now, although I am putting this out as blanket statements, there are always exceptions to the rules. You can be around specific behavior and remain grounded in who you are. From my experience, I hung around people that cursed a lot, which is especially prevalent in my profession, and I found myself dropping F-bombs more. When I hung around people who drank a lot, I drank more. I also have hung around people that engaged in marijuana, and eventually, I tried it. At 17, I took a pull, which confirmed that it was not for me. I was dating a guy who smoked, and I asked him to try it. He was hesitant initially but gave me a pull, and one pull was enough. Thankfully, I did not like how it made me feel and immediately knew it was not for me. Since both my parents suffered from addiction, I made a conscious effort to be careful of what I engaged in for fear of addiction. I remember being very young and the doctor telling my sister and me that because our parents struggled with addiction, it would make us more susceptible to addiction. I don't know if this was a scare tactic not to do drugs or the truth, but it stuck with me.

Who you surround yourself with plays a part in the person you become or the habits you pick up. While there is no one-size-fits-all when it comes to this, I can say with certainty that who you spend time with will play out in your behaviors. When we are with friends, we tend to let our guard down, and this is when it becomes easy for the habits of others to rub off on us. You are in your comfort zone, and it's easy for things to creep in when you are comfortable. When I moved to Maryland in 2005, I met a new group of peers through my job. This new group became my roll dawgs, as we painted the town red as a group of twenty-something-year-olds. I was 25 and had finally moved out of my hometown, The Bronx, New York (BX Stand up). During that time, I picked up smoking Black and Mild cigars. I had casually tried one while drinking with my friends, and the habit stuck. I had managed to go 25 years without smoking, and in a few months, I had picked up the habit without giving it a second thought. First Corinthians 15:33 says, "Do not be deceived; bad company ruins good morals." In no way am I insinuating that these group of friends were bad company. What I am saying is if you are not mindful of the company you keep, it has the potential to cause you to sway on your moral standard of living. However, many positives came with my group of friends as well. They were all highly motivated individuals interested in investments, owned property, were business owners, and actively pursued their undergraduate education.

Coming from NYC, the superficial layers of showing you had money were represented through your materialistic items, primarily clothing. I remember taking my son to daycare in the finest of leathers. My son had every timberland boot, Sean John outfit, Jordan, and

Polo. I would look around his classrooms, and his classmates wore Walmart sweatsuits and skippy sneakers. However, their parents were homeowners and investors. They did not wear their money; they made moves with it. This experience changed my thought process and caused me to rethink how I was spending my money. Eighteen months after moving to Maryland at 26, I purchased my first home. The power of surrounding yourself with the right people is undeniable. I hope I am always in the midst of people who can motivate me to higher performance levels, and I can do the same for those who consider me a friend or part of their Fav 5.

My grandmother would also say that you can't rise above the company you keep. That statement is in direct alignment with showing me your company. She would often say these statements within the same conversation to drive home the point of actively choosing your friends. In adult life, I have become selective about the people I allow in my life. Within a few interactions, I can decide whether this person is a good fit for the friend zone. Now, it's not that cut and dry, and I'm not reviewing resumes before bringing you into my circle. As a matter of fact, I'm not even actively conducting an elimination round. However, during our conversations, a few statements may cause me to raise an eyebrow and decide you will not go on to the next round of friendship. You will remain in the associate category.

I am very sensitive to how people treat their children. We can't be friends if your actions show that you do not prioritize your children. If you are still with the drama or always ready to engage in physical activity if someone looks at you for too long, we can't be friends. Calling your children derogatory names, we can't be friends. A bit judgy? Perhaps, but that type of behavior resonates with me. If every other word is a cuss word, especially as a woman, it is cringy. Now to be dropped from my friend zone is not a huge loss. Most of the time my circle is just my kids and me. But the older I get the more critical it is for me to protect my peace. Proverbs 12:20 tells us that "Whoever walks with the wise becomes wise, but the companion of fools will suffer harm." Who are you walking with? Who is in your Fav 5? In the words of Julia May Hill, "Show me your company, and I will tell you who you are."

It's a Mighty Poor Rat That Only Has One Hole

*T*his statement always brings a little smirk to my face. My grandmother would use this statement to refer to putting your everything into one area. This was usually in the context of relationships and dating at a young age. She was married once and never remarried after that. She alleged her husband was a philanderer and often stayed out or came in late from his escapades with different women. After her divorce from him, she decided she would never marry again. A rat with one hole is in congruence with the eggs in one basket statement. I have applied this statement to my professional and personal life. It is very important to diversify yourself in all aspects. Being a one-trick pony is not always productive. Diversity can open different opportunities for you and avoid pigeonholing into one area.

In my personal life, specifically relationships, I have avoided having only one hole to protect myself emotionally. I know what you are thinking, but you're mistaken. I am not speaking of being a serial dater or a cheater. I am referencing never making one person my everything. Have you ever met someone who lived and breathed the air of the person they dated? They lived a life that was entirely based on another person. I have most certainly met people like this. There is nothing wrong with this per se, but I will say when the relationship ends, the person is completely lost. Their entire being is wrapped up in the other person, and without them, they don't know how to move forward. I have experienced some bad break ups, but never to the point where I couldn't pick myself up and move forward with life. My thoughts went to that person I had recently broken up with, but it was not debilitating. I moved on with life in such a manner that others kept asking me if I was okay. They couldn't believe I was okay with the breakup and moving forward with life as if nothing had happened. Most people don't understand that when they see the breakup of a relationship, they don't see the process. The breakup occurred way before the actual and final breakup. There may have been baby breakups and distancing between the two, and eventually, they found themselves at the final showdown.

After experiencing the devastating loss of my mother, very few things could emotionally shake me. I got dealt a huge blow, and as I mentioned earlier, my coping mechanism was busying myself. So, of course, I have dealt with breakups in the same manner. I kept busy and moved on. The funny thing is I never did any of this intentionally. I was programmed to move this way; as an adult, it happened instinctively. A bad event would take place, I would take a moment to grieve, and then it was on to the next thing. It worked; my process was error-proof for many years. Although I later learned this was not a healthy way of coping, I feel this mode of dealing with grief saved me.

Back to the original statement regarding one hole in the context of relationships. Being in love is beautiful, but with my success rate, I've quickly learned that love isn't going to be forever. As a result, I've always been very timid about giving my entire heart. As I type this, I realize this could be a vicious cycle. Unwilling to give my heart in its entirety, I never fully receive the love I seek due to my lack of vulnerability. Men have told me that I've dated that I can be cold or act like a dude. I've always attributed my rough disposition to being from up north… THE BX!! (I couldn't resist myself). The majority of us northern females have a bit of a rough exterior. As I'm peeling away the layers, I realize the reason for my disposition in relationships is multi-faceted. For starters, every inkling of vulnerability was stripped away from me during my first adult relationship, which involved a lot of abuse. I remember sharing with him some of my most intimate thoughts. I told him about the actual cause of my mother's death. This was something I did not tell anyone growing up. Out of embarrassment, I would tell most people she passed away from cancer. I was too ashamed to tell people the truth out of fear of being judged. He took my innermost secret and turned it around on me. He would say hurtful things such as, "That's why your mother died of AIDS." This hurt me to my core. How could he betray me like this? He would remind me that I didn't have anyone who would be there for me. I learned earlier that you couldn't share everything with everyone through his words. What was the purpose? They would only use it to manipulate you later. Keep it to yourself; no one cares anyway. While there is some truth in this thought process, it is not entirely true. They are people who care and who will not use your words to manipulate them. The key is using discernment before sharing the things you hold dear to you.

In any event, these early formative years of adulthood shaped how I moved forward in my relationships. Coupled with the fact that I never received therapy after I left the abusive relationship, I was a hot mess. In my immediate next relationship, I was on edge. That relationship had its ups and downs. I don't believe I've ever dated someone that competitive to this day. He wasn't physically abusive, but he sure did a number on my self-esteem. For one, I believe he honestly felt he was too attractive for me. He never came out and said the words, but I just felt it. As I reflect, it may have been me and where I was in life. I didn't feel attractive; I felt worthless. I wasn't happy with where I was in life at the time. He had three baby mothers at 26 (Flag on the play), who were all fair-skinned. I thought to myself, I don't look anything like these other women. Did this guy want to be with me? My son's father constantly reminded me no one would ever want me with a child, and I began to believe this. Thank God for living because life has shown me otherwise. Plenty of men will date a woman who has children from a previous relationship. But at twenty, I believed what he said to be true.

Applying the rat and one hole has not been effective in my relationships. However, it was self-preservation and effective for me at a place in my life when I needed to feel safe. In never giving 100% of my heart, I have sabotaged relationships with people who earnestly cared about me. Use discernment and give your heart freely when you deem that person worthy. In my grandmother's context, I agree that young people should experience life and not limit their options early. Your early years are to live life freely and explore all your options. So many people commit at a young age when they are not ready for that level of commitment. Sometimes this works, and other times it can cause damage to someone you genuinely care about. In my professional life, diversifying has never been bad, and I am a strong proponent of having multiple holes. You will know what is best for you, and the threshold of whether you've made the right decision will be based on the results it yields. But when it comes to certain areas of your life, remember, it is a mighty poor rat that has only one hole.

Pray About It

I remember bringing the most important decisions to my grandmother and asking for her input. I would ask my grandmother what she thought I should do, and time after time, she would tell me to pray about it. I would immediately become frustrated and ask her again what she thought I should do. She would respond with the same answer "Pray about it.". If I told her I already did, she would ask, "Well what did he say?" This would frustrate me even more, and I would respond with, "Forget it." I couldn't understand why it was so difficult for her to realize that I simply needed her input. I needed her to give me some direction or what she thought would be the best course of action. If I told her I needed her input, she would say to me that I never listened to her anyway since I knew everything. That lady could really pluck my nerves, and I'm sure she felt that same way about me.

My grandmother always told people how hard-headed I was, and I thought I knew everything. Her favorite thing to say about me was "See Jessica, you can't just tell her it's raining outside, and she believes you, she has to go outside get wet and then come back inside and get an umbrella." She would also say "You can't tell her just the window is broken, the whole house got to fall in on her for her to believe you." These were the examples she used to illustrate how hardheaded and stubborn I was. I did not believe myself to be that stubborn or hardheaded. I'm not sure why the old lady, as she sometimes referred to herself, told those stories about me. In any event, asking for advice concerning major decisions could be tasking with her. She always directed me to seek counsel from God. She assured me that he would know what was best for me.

Earlier in life, I couldn't receive this idea of consulting God to provide answers to my real-world problems. I barely knew how to discern the voice of God (Something I still struggle with). How do I know the voice of God versus my voice and wants? In the bible, there appeared to be clear signs such as a burning bush or an angel interceding on God's behalf. But today, the messages are not that cut and dry, at least not for me. I realize that God gives us free will and choice, but how do I know what he wants for my life? Those questions always loomed whenever she told me to pray about life woes or significant decision points. When I was purchasing my first home, I found myself overwhelmed with the entire process. There was grandma again telling me to pray about it. In all fairness, she also told me when I walked into my home; I would know it was the right one. She was right about that part; the moment I walked into my house, I knew it was the right fit for my son and me. However, I needed answers from her, and she kept providing referrals to God, to who I wasn't entirely sure if he was responding. I had yet to learn to listen to him. I didn't understand God's language and how he talks to us or shall I say me.

God's communication will not always look the same for everyone. Gods' messages or communication may appear to us via dreams; there may be multiple confirmations of a message you heard or one word. God can use several vessels to get your attention. Before embarking upon this journey to write this book, the word transition kept coming up. I wrote the word in my journal after an argument with someone I was dating; the next week my sister sent me a YouTube message about being in a transitional phase. The same week that I wrote the word in my journal that following Thursday, my women's group weekly message touched upon transitioning. There is a belief that the appearance of something three times is confirmation. After the third time, I took heed to where I was in life, and the next question for me became transitioning to what. I still haven't 100% figured that part out, but I know God is moving me to another place in my life. I'm not the same person I was two months ago or a week ago.

When it came to the decisions in my life, I've always consulted with multiple people for feedback. Most times, I still did what I wanted to do after receiving all types of advice (I guess that's what my grandmother meant when she said hardheaded). Often the WHAT I wanted always won, and my decisions looked different from the advice that was given by others. Now here's a message when it comes to consulting. Be cognizant of who you take your troubles to; every listening ear is not a helping hand. Some people you confide in do not have your best interest at heart. Some people don't like to rock the boat, so they will cosign on just about anything you say. Some people want to hear your woes so that they can transcribe them word for word to someone else. Some people secretly pray for your downfall and love that you're not currently winning. They applauded you openly, but secretly they were tired of hearing the success stories. Some are too consumed with themselves and cannot even begin to focus on your issues.

Have you ever begun to tell someone a problem, and they one-up you with their problem? You start to tell them about your week and before you can fully tell them what happened to you, they are responding with, "If you think that's something? Let me tell you about MY week." I've convinced myself that those people don't even realize they're doing it. Because I despise this behavior so much, I am conscious not to do it to others when they express their problems to me. Part of communication is exchanging ideas and finding things that are relatable to what the other person is talking about. However, there are times when you must hold off on your story of when he cheated on you and listen to your friend and empathize. These people place the focus on themselves and what they are experiencing rather than being fully emotionally available to the person in need. There is an art to communication. Timing and reading cues are everything. Granted, please do not misunderstand what I'm saying because there should be an exchange of experiences in communication. Knowing when to bring up your situation is essential in communication.

The best advice about significant decisions in our life comes by first taking it to the man upstairs, God. Consult with him first because as my grandmother would also say, "There is nothing new under the sun for him." There is no problem that you can bring to him that he has not seen nor heard. After you have consulted with God, be still and listen to what he is saying to you. As I said earlier, those answers can come to you in several ways. It may be the pastor's message, a scripture in the bible, a coworker, or a friend. You never know who God will use to get your attention.

But the most important thing when you encounter situations in your life or transitional points is to "Pray about it."

The Hand That
Rocks the Cradle
Rules the World

One can never undermine the importance of parenthood. When my grandmother made the statement the hand that rocks the cradle rules the world, she was emphasizing the burden of motherhood. In search of another word for burden, I came up with grave responsibility. Although my grandmother used this statement specifically in reference to motherhood, I will take it a step further and say parenthood. As parents, it is incumbent upon us to understand our role in developing future leaders and game-changers. The language we use, the non-verbal lessons we provide, and the absence or presence of a parent all send a resounding message to our children and shape their development. As a parent,

I've learned firsthand that the messages I don't give are louder than those I do.

Last year I had a conversation with my oldest son about his plans for the next phase of his life. He was transitioning into adulthood as a college graduate. We talked about career goals and family planning. He told me he wanted to conceive his first child around 27-ish. My next question was what his plans concerning marriage were. I needed to know where that fits into his timeline. "When do you plan on getting married?" He responded that he hadn't thought about that part. "Well, fathering children should follow marriage son." Things don't always work out that way, but this should be the gold standard. I realized that while this is a message that I consistently communicated to both of my children, it was the exact opposite of what he had witnessed. Not just in our home but within our family and the African American community. I am not saying it doesn't happen in other communities; however, it is prevalent in the community which he directly observes. He had watched a long lineage of single parenthood in our family. The women in my family did it with such grace that it almost did not seem problematic. However, the absence of a parent has long-term effects on children and the parent that is left holding the bag.

A male child raised by a single mother will take one or two approaches. They will ensure that they do everything possible to bring their children up in a two-family home, or they will be more likely to walk away because they saw their "strong mother" raise children by themselves. Due to their family dynamics, they believe the woman they have procreated with should be able to do the same as their mother without issue. This is not bible or research-proven, just my personal beliefs.

Absentee parents teach so many lessons about life that is unbeknownst to them. One of the most important lessons their absence teaches children is that it is okay to walk away from their responsibilities. Their absence can also bring about a myriad of emotions, particularly anger, distrust, and self-esteem issues. I have witnessed firsthand the impact of an absentee father on my children. It begins with questioning why the other parent isn't interested in them. It turns into hurt and boils over into anger. Eventually, the child shuts down and attempts to ignore that part of their life altogether.

The phrase I would begin to hear is "I don't care" when it came to issues concerning their dads. I realized that when they said this, they were in fact saying they did care, but it hurt too much to deal with. So, they would use avoidance to remove any emotional attachment in this area.

Filling the void was impossible for me as a woman because no matter how hard I tried, I could never be their fathers. Knowing this, I never tried to be their dad; I was simply the best mom I could be. I dealt with their void by ensuring my kids were always involved in activities and kept the lines of communication open to talking. Activities for my boys generally involved church, sports, and family outings. The problem with sports is there is a lot of male representation. This is a good and bad thing. It is good because they need to see positive representation. The downside was that it constantly reminded them of what they lacked when all the other children's dads were present.

I dealt with similar emotions as a child; however, I would say my situation was a little better; hear me out. My mother passed when I was nine, and it hurt when I saw children with their moms. Although the hurt existed, there was no one to blame because it was physically impossible for her to be here. I didn't experience anger towards her as I did not have to watch her live a life that did not include me. When it came to my father, he was in and out of jail and could not be present. I understood this concept and believed that he would've been there if he had been out. He proved this to me through his actions. When he was out of jail, he always made a full-on effort to spend time with us. With my children, there were no barriers to their fathers spending time with them, no extenuating circumstances. All barriers were self-imposed and fabricated reasons why they couldn't make a concerted effort to spend time with them. It was a lot of woes is me, and I'm barely surviving.

Children need both parents. What do I'm barely surviving mean to a child? It means absolutely nothing. It means my life circumstances are more important than being a part of your life. My issues take priority over you. My kids only wanted their presence. They did not want their money, only their time. I realize it is hard to look out for someone else when you are barely above water but isn't that what parenthood is about? You make the sacrifices; you are willing to lose for them to win. You accept the sleepless nights, forfeit your weekends for basketball tournaments, smile when you're hurting on the inside, be the strength when you are too weak for yourself, and pour into your children with everything you've got. That's what it means when my grandmother said the hand that rocks the cradle rules the world. You do all this and pray that your efforts have contributed significantly to tomorrow's leaders. When it is all said and done, you are prayerful that you have raised productive members of society who will avoid the mishaps you fell victim to. You expect this because of the sacrifices you've made for them and the lessons you have taught them along the way. Parents, rock those cradles ever so gently. Rock those cradles with meticulous attention to detail. Rock those cradles until your arms are tired (taking breaks as needed for self-care), and they will positively rule the world!

An Ounce of Prevention is Worth a Pound of Cure

*W*hat is harder? Taking the precautionary steps to prevent something or fixing it once you've messed up. I would say the latter of the two is more challenging. In the post-world of Covid, many have a deeper understanding of how important it is to take precautionary methods. We all dawned masks, some under protest, others willingly conceded to the new norm. Some of us took it a step further and were vaccinated, hoping not to catch Covid. Others were threatened with loss of jobs before they begrudgingly took the vaccine. These were all preventive measures in the hopes of not being attacked by a virus we initially knew very little about. The lucky ones have managed to escape the virus for the past three years, while others have been infected multiple times. I belong to the latter group. I took precautionary measures; however, my efforts proved futile. At times I was careless in my interactions with others. I believe this carelessness led to getting covid twice, but for the most part, I was safe. Life will surprise you in this way sometimes. You do everything right, but the few times you let your guard down, it happens. It only takes one time.

Growing up my grandmother would say, "A ounce of prevention is worth a pound of cure." when I was doing something she considered foolish with dire consequences. Whether it was not bundling up during the winter or not taking my allergy medicine mid-spring with a high pollen count, she would chastise me with those words. Verbally I would say, "Okay grandma", but in all actuality, I was blowing her off. Depending on how she felt, she would follow up and say, "It's better to light a candle than to curse the darkness." Lawdt, I get it!! But if she still felt she was still not getting through to me she would say in frustration "You don't believe S**t stink." At that point, I would know she was pretty serious and comply with whatever she was demanding to appease her. I couldn't understand her frustration with me doing something that could only harm me. However, I completely understand this as a parent of an adult and teenage son. I believe I OVERSTAND it.

Your emphasis on your child taking the necessary precautionary methods for whatever danger arises stems from your genuine love and concern for them. Unfortunately, I had to become a parent for the light-bulb to go off. Why is it that some things in life we must experience on our own? How much easier would life be if we only listened to our elders or those with lived experience? Proverbs 22:3 tell us the wise see danger ahead and avoid it, but fools keep going and get into trouble. We are all fools when we are young. There were so many paths that I continued down despite seeing the danger that lay ahead. This often happened to me with the people I decided to call friends or boyfriends. I made these decisions against a strong urging from my grandmother that the person did not have my best interest at heart or, in her exact words, "Do not mean you no good." Parents have this sensor that can detect which friends in your circle do not mean you well. It's like a bio scanner that can read the person and flashes a good or bad sign. You will get the next visual reference point if you are into fantasy movies.

One of my favorite movies was the original Charlie and the Chocolate Factory. I remember a scene where Willy Wonka is showing the machine, which determines which piece of candy is good or bad via a scan. Parents have this knack for doing the same thing with your friends. With hindsight being twenty-twenty you learn later in life that your parents are usually right regarding such matters. So, where am I going with all of this? Many of the things we experience in life are preventable self-inflicted wounds. The knowledge is out there for all life's problems if we take the time to listen or research. As my grandmother would say "There is nothing new under the sun."

Some of us find ourselves haphazardly making significant decisions in our life without doing the initial research or consultation. Most of these decisions concern personal matters because when it comes to career decisions, it generally makes more sense to do your homework. So, we do our homework before making any major career decisions. However, we tend to skip this step regarding personal matters. Ignoring these steps can have significant consequences in developing your relationships with other people and your self-development. One thing you should do before entering any situation is a pulse check on yourself. What level are you vibrating on? Where are you currently? Where you are determines who and what you attract to you.

In a recent women's meeting, we discussed Genesis, when God went into the garden and called for Adam and Eve. God asked, "Where are you?" I always attributed this question to God asking about their physical location. What was revealed to me is that God is all-knowing, he knew exactly where they were. Essentially, he was asking where they were emotionally and spiritually. Where you are spiritually determines what you attract and the things you entertain. When your spirit is in alignment with God or a higher purpose, you won't be able to remain in certain situations. I often hear people say they are vibrating on a high frequency or speak about their energy. I used to think what energy are they talking about? Sometimes things become cliché within the culture, and you hear people using the same terminology. It is used to the point of overkill where internally, I am screaming; I get it you are "woke". Energy is a real thing; we all possess energy. This energy can fluctuate as we move through different phases of our lives or even the day. Now, if your energy is all over the place daily, you may need to consult someone. Energy, coupled with the environments you place yourself in, can attract the right or wrong things based on where you are spiritually. If you are vibrating on a low frequency, it doesn't make sense to surround yourself with others in the same place. However, we find ourselves doing this and can't understand why we are stuck in a perpetual rut.

It's essential to have people who can relate to what we are going through but be mindful of whether they are still stuck there. As I've gotten older, I have consciously tried to surround myself with people I could learn something from or who could pour into my spirit. I remember one Sunday while attending a church in Georgia, the pastor said it was easy to catch someone's sickness or negative energy. You sit next to someone who is sick and the next thing you know you are sick as well. This painted a clear picture for me on how easy it is to pick up negativity or things that are harmful to you. However, it's challenging to catch someone's good health, it is impossible.

Be careful who you call on when you are not at your best. Pay attention to how you feel after speaking with that person. Do you feel uplifted, or are you just as angry? Are you motivated and can now see your way out of the situation, or do you feel just as stuck? Did they speak life over your situation or death? Now, I am not suggesting that you only have friends that will rub your back and not give you the real. However, I am saying to get you some friends who can keep it 100%, restore, and empower you once the conversation is done. If I am still angry and ready to bust the windows out of his car after our discussion, maybe that friend is not the one to call when I'm upset. Although, these friends do come in handy at times. Sometimes you need that friend that says, "Cool, tonight we ride at dusk." I'm joking….. maybe. Having a friend or two who are about that life isn't always a bad thing.

Back to the original intent, prevention comes in different forms. Let me readjust that statement; how you employ prevention will vary. Although how it is used may change, utilizing that ounce of prevention is imperative for long-term success. Prevention can be heeding the advice of others, following your gut instinct, seeking counsel with those who have already traveled your path, or, most notably and foremost, consulting with God before any major movements. God will be your preventive medicine for the stressors of life. As God becomes your preventive medicine you will see the outcome of your decisions change because you've consulted with him before you took the first step. Through consultation with God, he will order your steps. Some of us forget to consult on the front end, and then we want God to fix it on the backend after we've messed it up. Guilty as charged! I've placed myself in some challenging situations and after the fact I've tried to pray my way out. "Lord, if you get me out of this, I promise I won't do it again." Life and experience have taught me to always place God on the front, middle, and back end. That's the wisdom that comes with living a little. So put on the whole armor of God and allow him to be your preventive medicine to life. As grandma would say, "An ounce of prevention is worth a pound of cure."

A Fool and His Money
Will Soon Part

I have repeated these words to myself so many times after spending my money unwisely. Goodness, what was I thinking? I'm sure we've all spent money on things that we immediately regretted. It may have been buying a bottle at the club with the 100% markup, those new Gucci shoes, an expensive meal that you could've prepared for half the price at home or another pair of shoes you did not need. Whatever it was, you kicked yourself for making such a foolish purchase. Now sometimes, these things are a part of our self-care. There is nothing wrong with treating yourself to the things that you like. However, the biggest thing is ensuring you can afford the things you purchase and the intent behind the purchase. Are you buying these items because they are things you generally like, or is it to impress others? Where is your heart? Are you purchasing these items thinking, "They are going to be sick when they see me in this." or are you thinking, "I deserve this, and it will look beautiful on me."

Coming from a place of not always having access to the things we want in life can create an unhealthy desire for them once they become within reach. Growing up in the city, wealth or status was attributed to what you wore. The type of sneakers you wore, the name brand of the clothing, jewelry, and hairstyles all contributed to your social status. In middle school, the most popular children were generally the ones with the latest fashions. At least, that was the minimal requirement to enter the popular crew. After that, your personality or ability to fight would determine how long you stayed there. We see the most expensive designer labels within some of the most poverty-stricken communities. We see individuals operating slightly above the poverty line attempting to emulate those in the entertainment industry that have the financial means to purchase high-end items. We witness an artist who has come from bare-bones situations reach a certain level of stardom and financial success, and because they did not have access to money, they now overly display their money. This display is witnessed through jewelry, clothing, luxurious cars, the flashing of money on social media, and footwear. There is nothing wrong with buying nice clothes and exclusive jewelry, especially if you have the money to spend. I'm referencing those who don't have it. I'm talking about the ones who buy in excess but own nothing. I'm sure some of you know exactly who I am speaking of. I was one of those people buying in access, using my best friend's Visa and Mastercard to pay, and doing all this while accruing high-interest rates.

Granted, as African American people, we are flagrant in our style. We can take nothing and make it look like something. We will put a razzle-dazzle on it as we emulate the lifestyles of those who have. The people in the industry have the financial means, or at least I'm assuming they do for their flashy lifestyle. However, many of us live a high-end lifestyle but don't necessarily have the finances to match it. Credit cards are being maxed out to maintain an image or a lifestyle that your bank account cannot support. If you come into wealth but don't have the knowledge to manage it properly, eventually, you will lose it. Additionally, you will never get to a place of wealth if every dollar coming in is going out to support an image.

Wisdom and knowledge used interchangeably in this paragraph will determine how long you maintain a financial status or get to a higher socio-economic status. What happens when you have obtained the finances, but the mentality remains the same? How many individuals have quickly come into a fortune and filed for bankruptcy years later because they mismanaged their funds or didn't pay their taxes? How many of our young rappers are gunned down because they've failed to realize they can't move in the same manner or in the same areas they previously moved in? They lacked wisdom. Wisdom will allow you to see that some of those same individuals that were once your friends now loathe what you have. Wisdom will give you the foresight that there are people who have never met you yet are looking for an opportunity to catch someone like you slipping. If you are not proactive in how you move, it will create the segway for someone else to establish themselves. You don't have to be famous to see what jealousy and envy can do. Those two emotions can cause people to want what you have, and some will act on the impulse to take it

I have always enjoyed going to the casino and playing roulette or slot machines. Initially, when I started playing, I would win a few dollars; it could be as low as thirty dollars, and I would take off running like I stole something. The more I continued to go to the casino, the higher the win I was looking for. The thirty bucks were no longer enough to celebrate a win and go home. That's the hook and sink. Once they give you a big win, the little ones are never sufficient. After spending my last little coin chasing a win, I would head home, repeatedly mumbling that a fool and his money will soon part. It is challenging to win in a game never designed for you to win. The intent is to get you hooked. Even when you win, you are losing because at some point, you will be back to reinvest what you previously won. I was the fool in the casino parting with my money.

In many places throughout the bible where fools are referenced. Why is that? Do you think God believes a fool deserves biblical recognition? Through the parables or reference points to fools; God is giving us a blueprint for life. Here are a few things the bible tells us about fools. They start fights, are easily upset, believe everything he reads, love to talk but hate to listen, are fiercely independent, make light of sin, and hate their mother. The above characteristics of a fool can be found in proverbs. How many people do you know if going by the above characteristics is a fool? There is a popular song by a group called the Main Ingredient entitled "Everybody Plays the Fool." We have all been a fool at some point or another in our lives, however, through wisdom we don't have to stay there. Through financial literacy, we can hold onto our money. Speaking with individuals who have started with nothing and now live in abundance, we can learn common pitfalls. We can ensure our money will not depart us through tithing and not stealing from God. Are you the fool? If you are, you don't have to stay there. Staying is a choice because the knowledge is available if you seek it.

A Frog Will Praise
His Own Pond Even if
There is No Water in It

know you are looking at this chapter's title and
scratching your head. No worries, growing up, it
took me a while to get this one. I would laugh because it
sounded funny and then wonder what this even meant.
It was even harder to ensure I was driving home the
message to my readers in a manner that made sense.
Whenever my grandmother said this to me, I immediately got an image of a little frog sitting on a lily pad in
a pond with barely enough water in it for him to swim.
But the frog was just as content and was croaking his
heart away. No one could take away the frog's joy because he was satisfied with what he had. So much so
that he bragged to anyone within earshot. As I further

thought about it, I almost became envious of the frog; what peace he must have experienced to be so content in what others may have considered dreadful circumstances. The frog could barely swim in the pond he bragged about, yet there he was, croaking for all to hear.

There are several ways to look at this. First, as mentioned above, we can admire the ability of those who can be content in where they are in the present. Perhaps the frog is content because he knows the potential of the pond. He may know that on the horizon is a storm that will last for a couple of hours and restore his pond. He knows that his current situation is not permanent but a temporary setback. Therefore, he croaks and sings praises amid his shortcomings. What a blessing to have faith while going through our biggest storm. Some of us would have given up and set out to find another pond the moment things started to look uncertain. We would've panicked and, out of fear, uprooted everything to find refuge elsewhere. This frog possessed patience, personal courage, and faith. Some of you probably think enough about the frog, and that's okay. But this guy is speaking to someone else who mastered the art of giving thanks in areas where others cannot begin to see the light. They cannot open their mouths and give thanks when life is challenging. They are easily discouraged and led astray. It's easy to give praise when things are going as planned. It is easy to give praise when you are winning. But can you give praise when the bough breaks, and you have nothing left?

That was the positive outlook of the frog. The other way of looking at this is the frog is arrogant and conceited. There he is with his loud croaking about his pond and disturbing others. He pays no attention to what others may feel or believe about his circumstance. He is absorbed with himself; no matter how bad his situation is, he will try to convince others it is the best thing and prime real estate. He lives in a world of illusions and grandiose and wants others to believe that things are as he sees them. Proverbs 27:2 tells us, "Let another praise you, and not your own mouth; a stranger and not your own lips." While we should be confident in who we are, we should never begin to praise ourselves to the point of bragging. Have you ever met someone like this? Talking to them is draining; these people is constantly singing high praises of themselves. They talk about what they've accomplished and give you their five-year plan.

All without you ever asking for any of this. Some people do the same with their children. How's little Bobby doing... 20 minutes later, they are still telling you about all their kid has accomplished. This is great, and I love a good kid success story, but we all know the ones that are overkill.

Another perspective to examine is how you respond to the frog. Where you are in life determines how you interpret and respond to where the frog is. Are you in the fullness of life? Are you at a place where you remain unphased no matter how much the frog is croaking? Some people become frustrated when others praise themselves, especially when they believe that person is telling lies. They will be annoyed and frustrated with the constant attempts to convince you of other than what you see with your own eyes. They can see the pond, which doesn't match what you're saying. Some will be empathetic and feel sorry for the frog. "What a poor frog that he must try and convince us that life is good." When they encounter the frog with an almost empty pond, others will be like Jobs' friends in the bible and tell the frog to curse God and move on. Others will distance themselves from him because they are tired of the constant self-praise. Some friends may even believe the frog's beliefs and become jealous of his dry pond. Although the frog does not have much, some will want what he has.

How we respond to things will always be traced back to where we are in our journey. The story or analogy of the frog can be interpreted from several angles. You have the frog itself and how he views his situation. You have how others view his situation. Then you have how others respond to the frog. Whether you are the frog singing high praises for your borderline dry pond or the ones who can hear the croaking, how you respond will be determined by where you are mentally and spiritually.

Nothing Happens
Before it's Time

Throughout my life, I can remember running home from school to tell my grandmother some great news, and as an adult, I would do the same until she passed. Anything significant that happened in my life, whether it was for my children or me, I ran or later rushed to the phone to tell grandma. Funny, when I said tell, it also reminded me of how I was a tattle teller or what they call a snitch nowadays to my grandmother. My twin sister hated it. As much as I told on my sister, she always held it down for me. Awww, I almost feel bad, emphasis on almost, but I love you sis. In any event, I would share the news with my grandmother, and after congratulating me, she would follow up with, "Nothing happens before its time." I would agree with her, but I never really went deeper into understanding what it meant. I didn't realize the true power of these statements until I was older and found myself saying them to myself or my children. This particular statement is all about God's infinite and impeccable timing.

Timing is everything. When we think about living things, they all mature in their own time. They never reach full maturity before it is time; it is a process. Ecclesiastes 3:11 tell us, "He made everything beautiful in its time." Consider if you will the gift of life; it takes 40 weeks for an embryo to develop into a full-term baby. It's a slow and deliberate process, with each week representing a step in the developmental phase. All of this is for a reason. Time allows for things to grow into what they were designed to do. However, as humans, we always try to rush the hand of time. Our society wants immediate results; patience is a virtue in this day and age. I remember growing up and having to wait for movies that were recently in the box office to be shown on T.V. Now a movie leaves the theater, and what seems like the next month, it's on your home streaming applications. Better yet, if you have a jailbroke fire stick, you can get it at the same time it's in the theater.

This is without the people standing up and shouting in the background like the old bootleg DVDs. I don't know anything about that; it's just what I heard (lol). Nonetheless, we want instant results with everything.

I didn't grow up with a microwave. We had a convection oven and the stove. Those were your two options for warming up your food. I hated this as I would go to some of my friends' homes, and they would throw stuff in the microwave, and wallah it was done. I desired those things, and I purchased one as soon as I got my first place. Now, I avoid using the microwave due to the radiation. Ephesians 5:15 tells us to look carefully how you walk, not as unwise but as wise, making the best use of the time. The Bible implies that the wise make the best use of time.

The wise do not rush time; instead, they respect the time and allow things to happen as they should. They still take a proactive stance regarding their time; however, they do not hurry along the hands of time. If we are patient and persistent, things will unfold precisely when they should. Has something ever happened, and you thought it was right on time? That's God's timing;

his time is never late. As the song says, he may not come when you want him to, but he's on time. Perhaps, you longed for a mate, a baby, a marriage, or a career and questioned when would be your time. For you, it seems as if things were happening for everyone else except you. Your frustration may have grown, and you may have even grown envious of watching others have what you wanted. When those things finally came to fruition for you, you realized that at the point in your life when you wanted those things, you weren't in a place to receive them.

I remember being a staff sergeant in the Army for what seemed like forever. Year after year, I would rush to see the promotion list. My battles would send me the blacklist, which was the list that someone managed to get their hands on before the official list was published. I would be disappointed for three almost four years. Eventually, I got to the point where I stopped focusing on promotion and began focusing on taking care of my Soldiers. I looked for ways to get them promoted and develop them as Soldiers. Promotion no longer consumed me, and then it happened. I was promoted to sergeant first class. I realized I needed those years to develop myself as a leader. I went from a sergeant to a staff sergeant in 8 months which was extremely fast. The valuable grooming that takes place when you become a sergeant could not fully take place in 8 months. The promotion did not come when I wanted it, but it came in congruence with God's timeline for my life.

I've learned over the years when there are things that I want, it is best to thank God for where I am and what I currently have. You can't receive more if you are not in a place of gratitude for what you have. I also pray for God to direct my path and have his way in all areas of my life. When I do this, I can truly let go and let God. What are you rushing the hands of time on? Have you given it to God? When you release it, you worry less about the when and learn to enjoy the now. I realize it's easier said than done, but anything you desire, you must release it to God and understand his timing. I am leaning on God and understanding that his timeline will never be the same. This doesn't mean that you stop working toward the goal. It just means understanding it may not happen when you want. It is essential to have patience and trust in the process. God's timeline may be earlier than yours or later. I did not expect to have my first son at 20 or the second at 27. Neither one of these was planned pregnancies, but many blessings came through my children. They came right on time; it wasn't my time, but I know God had a purpose for them in my life. My children became the motivation for every step I took afterward. As grandma said, "Nothing happens before its time."

God is Still on
The Throne

Whenever the world seemed upside down, my grandmother always reminded us that "God is still on the throne." It was a simple phrase, but it created such peace and calm in knowing that our heavenly father ultimately had the last say in whatever was happening in the world. In today's time, the world can be a very chaotic place. I gravitated away from watching the news for a long time due to the heaviness I immediately felt afterward. Everything seemed to scream doom and gloom. I had to control the things which I allowed into my space. Based on my career field, I must stay abreast of what is happening in the world, but I had to establish healthy boundaries. Reading the news versus watching television, where I was bombarded with unsolicited imagery, worked best for my mental health. I became selective with the news media outlets I selected. I elected neutral outlets and reported the news with little to no imposing of political viewpoints. Little adjustments such as these made all the difference in maintaining my energy. In your personal life, you may also need to set boundaries to create protected mental well-being for yourself.

God is still on the throne was a grounding statement for me. It was a gentle yet reassuring reminder that God was in control regardless of what was going on in the world. I knew that God took care of those who believed and trusted in him. Throughout my life, I have heard the following scripture multiple times "Train up a child in the way he should go, and when he is old, he will not depart from it." This quote comes from Proverbs 22:6 and emphasizes teaching our children how to live. My grandmother taught me how to live life in abundance through her actions and words. As a child or young adult, I couldn't always receive these lessons because I was consumed with living life on my terms. My terms were like most individuals in that age category have fun and deal with consequences later. However, her words never fleeted too far from me. They were always within me, urging me to make the hard right than the easy left.

We must have faith to truly believe that God is on the throne. Though life may test our faith daily, we must remain steadfast and hold the fort. Suffering domestic abuse at an early age, when I was most vulnerable, caused me to question many things. I never questioned God but pondered the why behind it all. I did not believe that God could cause such pain. That was not the type of God I served. However, I knew and acknowledged that my actions led me astray from his grace and covering. My faith allowed me to believe that my current situation was temporary and when the opportunity presented itself, I broke free. God will always remain a constant in my life. Although life may present some challenges and the outlook may be grim, "I will look towards the hills from whence cometh my strength." That's another scripture my grandmother would quote. If we believe that God is still on the throne, we will understand that all things in life are temporary. We know that no matter how bad things get, there is always hope through his presence.

The Fabric of Me

*I*n our home, tears weren't allowed; if you did cry, you were sent to the bathroom to get it all out, and then you could return when you had gathered yourself. Or, while crying, you would be told it was good for the soul and cleaned your eyes. However, you did not receive that shoulder to cry on. I remember coming home from school to find out my mother had passed away. My grandmother told us the news of my mother's passing very matter-of-factly. My sisters and I all went off to grieve in our own way. We didn't cry on one another or hug each other tightly. We all went into our own areas of the home and grieved. This started the path to how I dealt with grief or trauma. I dealt with it on my own, and I moved on. Crying wouldn't do much good, and life would keep moving forward. My grandmother, although stoic in her disposition, really had a heart of gold. I realized that she also never truly learned how to be vulnerable. Perhaps, at one point, she was vulnerable, and life quickly taught her that a vulnerable woman could not survive. My vulnerability was snatched away from me when I revealed the most sensitive parts of my story and had them thrown back in my face. Life quickly taught me that the vulnerable side of you was not to be shared.

Parenting has been one of the most challenging yet fulfilling roles that I have taken on. The idea that we bring these humans into this world and are charged with providing safety, protection, love, and guidance while simultaneously doing the same for ourselves is quite remarkable. While providing all these things, some of us still struggle with feeling loved, appreciated, and secure within ourselves. You're giving the things that you lack to someone else. That was me, pouring from an empty cup while creating an image of a full one. One of the last memories of my mother was her pouring into us through her words even when she had nothing left. It was my oldest sister's birthday. I imagine it was a cold day since my sister's birthday is in

February. The bell rang in the apartment, and it was my mother. We were all surprised that she was ringing the bell since last we knew, she was in the hospital. She would often leave the hospital dressed in nothing but her hospital robes and walk the street. The disease had begun to take over her mind. She hated being in the hospital just as much as we hated seeing her there. When she came upstairs, she had a black trash bag that contained random items. I remember a hubcap, some lunch meat, and other miscellaneous items. The one item that will forever remain with me is a single red rose. She reached into the bag, handed the rose to my sister, and said, "Happy Birthday." She remembered my sister's birthday; the disease had not stolen that from her. Later that night after my grandmother bathed her and provided her with some fresh clothes to sleep in. We all lay in the bed together, and I will never forget the words she said to us. She told us two things: "Whatever you do, get your education." and "Don't make the same mistakes I've made." She also made us promise to visit her at the cemetery every Mother's Day once she passed away. In her final moments, she was still giving, and those words remained with me forever.

My path has been highs and lows, crooked roads and straight ones, off-the-beaten paths, and on the well-traveled. God has been there through it all, carrying me at some points and walking beside me during others. But one thing I can say is that he never left me alone. In addition to God's ever presence, my grandmother has never left my side. Even after her departure at the age of 90, she stayed close through her words. Her words have guided me through some of the most tumultuous times. Her words have stung and cut so deep, but they were true. Her words have spoken life over me. There is power in the tongue. Which means there is power in the words we speak. You need to know this. We can speak life into and over our situations. I am grateful for the words spoken over me, and the words of encouragement others have given me.

By sharing some of those things that others have shared with me and experiences throughout my life, I hope to offer some encouragement to someone else. I hope you find a nugget for living the same way I have within these words. You can begin to speak your truth over others, and maybe someone will write a book based on the words you spoke to them. Through sharing some of my vulnerable moments, I hope you can realize that your story of triumph is a testimony to someone else. The words that aren't spoken are the ones that do not have the ability to impact. Speak your truth!

What I've learned in writing this book is that many of the phrases that my grandmother would say offered an opportunity for a deeper understanding of myself and the world around me. Through her words, I've lived and will continue to live. Her words have offered me confidence, courage, and a voice in her absence. We never fully recover from losing a loved one, but we learn how to adapt to our new normal. When you lose someone close to you, you never really lose them. They live on through their words and memories. Sometimes if you are lucky, they will send gentle reminders to let you know they are with you. In the early morning hours on the day of my promotion to Sergeant Major, I woke up at 5:55 am. When I looked up the meaning of this angel number, it meant that your guardian angel was looking out for you. It was no coincidence that I woke up precisely at 5:55 on such a monumental day. It was her way of saying she was still with me and celebrating right beside me.

When people leave our lives, their words still linger. The things they said, good or bad, resonate with us. I found healing in reliving the words my grandmother spoke to me. I discovered that even though she was no longer with me in human form, I held her closely through her words. I had so many revelations and new-found perspectives on living life. I knew that I wanted my grandmother's words to live on even after I was gone. It is my intent that through her words, some of you will unlock some of the lessons to living life in abundance. Through her words, I live!!

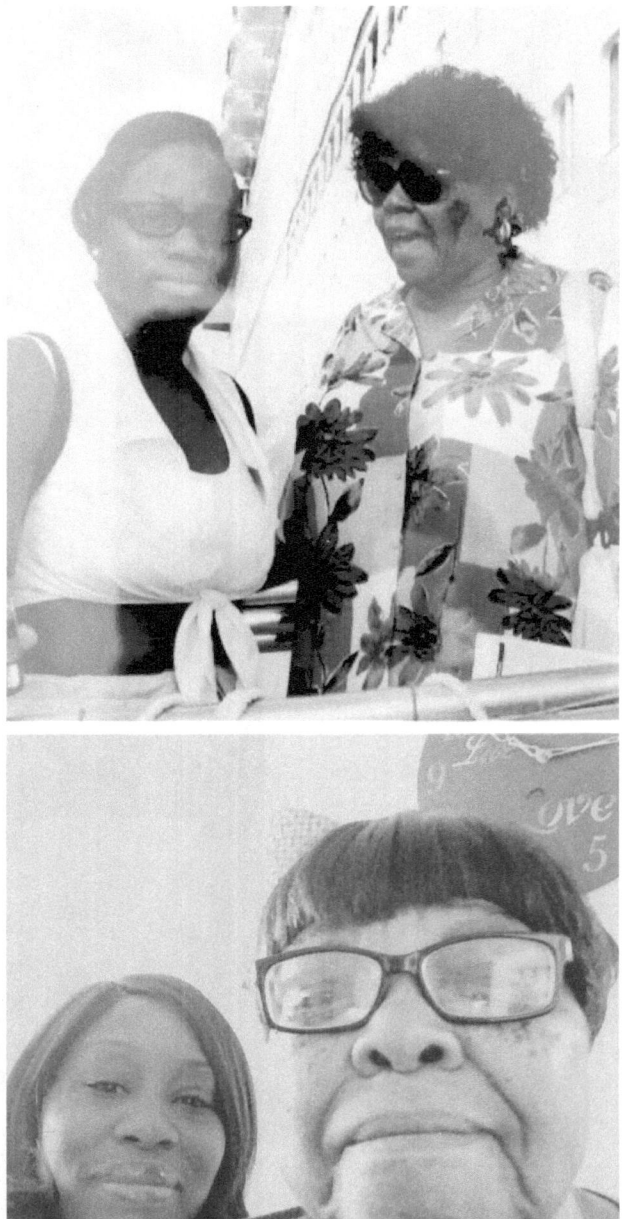

www.ingramcontent.com/pod-product-compliance
Lightning Source LLC
Chambersburg PA
CBHW020411130626
46549CB00006B/2517